"The Little Black Dress"

❧ Wounded Heart ~ Healing God ❧

Robyn B. Light ❤

WestBow
PRESS
A DIVISION OF THOMAS NELSON

Scripture taken from the Holy Bible, New International
Version®. Copyright © 1973, 1978, 1984 Biblica. Used
by permission of Zondervan. All rights reserved.

WestBow Press books may be ordered through booksellers or by contacting:

WestBow Press
A Division of Thomas Nelson
1663 Liberty Drive
Bloomington, IN 47403
www.westbowpress.com
1-(866) 928-1240

ISBN: 978-1-4497-1918-0 (sc)
ISBN: 978-1-4497-1919-7 (e)

Library of Congress Control Number: 2011931694

Printed in the United States of America

WestBow Press rev. date: 9/02/2011

"A friend loveth at all times..."

Proverbs 17:17(a)
King James Version

Given in Friendship:

To: _____

From: _____

Date: _____

_____

_____

_____

_____

_____

_____

_____

*"Dear friend, I pray that you may enjoy good health
and that all may go well with you, even as your soul is
getting along well."*

3 John 1:2
NIV

This book is dedicated to:

Janet Shockley
For playing dress up with me.
For understanding the pain and walking me through.

Vonda Goellner
For encouraging me to step outside my comfort zone.
For your example of a faith-filled life.

Wanda Lee
For patiently editing and reviewing this text.
For loving me no matter what.

Tawnya Eller
For gifting me with your prayers.
For being my encourager.

Janice Jiles
For comforting my veil of tears.
For holding on and never letting go.

Sonja Veile
For defining our friendship in a song.
For making music that touches the heart.

Meghan Behymer-Lindstrom
For my beautiful niece- thank you for your artful illustration
of "The Little Black Dress."
I love you around the world and then some.

Vickie Dalseg
For faithful hours of unending support.
For freely giving of your time, talents and love.

And…

To every woman who knows the pain of losing someone they love; and in the process losing sight of themselves - may each of you be blessed with cherished friends in whom Christ's love is reflected that you might recapture the truth of who you are in Him.

"The Little Black Dress"
Wounded Heart ~ Healing God

I stood silently at my kitchen sink washing a small plate that held the remnants of a half-eaten scrambled egg I'd tried to force down for dinner, when I heard the phone ring. I really wasn't feeling much like talking but hesitantly I answered, "Hello?"

"Are you home?" I heard my friend's enthusiastic voice ask. "Yes, I'm home." I replied. "Good, because I'm on my way over", she said; "I won't be there long but I should arrive in less than five minutes. Come to the front door."

"What's this all about?" I asked.

"Just wait, I'm almost there." She replied.

I walked to the dining room window and stared out toward the long road that led to the top of my driveway. I didn't really feel much like company but my friend didn't sound like she was going to take no for an answer. I just wanted to be left alone, to stew in my own sadness and sense of loss.

I didn't want to think. I didn't want to feel. I didn't want to try and engage in conversation. I didn't know what I wanted. I just knew that nothing was going to replace what I had lost and nothing was ever going to make me feel better about myself again.

❤

As I gazed into the distance I took a deep breath, hoping for a little relief from the ache in my heart. It was an awful feeling. Only someone who had experienced a terribly deep sense of loss could really understand the searing, gripping pain that pulsated through every inch of my being. He'd been gone over five months now but it still felt like it had happened only yesterday.

Looking beyond the trees, shrubs and flowers that blanketed our yard, thoughts of our life together kept running through my mind like water over the bumpy rocks in a river stream. So much good I thought, every one has rough times in their lives, but for the most part we had a wonderful life. Never in my wildest dreams could I have ever imagined that one day he would come home to tell me he was leaving. Our life together was over.

The first ten years of our marriage were sheer bliss. We had worked hard to set goals and make plans for our future. So often we excitedly spoke about how wonderful it was to literally watch each one of our dreams unfold.

The last two years had been different. We had struggled as one problem or tragedy followed another. It seemed life was fraught with family illnesses, surgeries and deaths. We questioned if life would ever return to a peaceful place where once again we would feel that same sense of calm we had when we were first married; whether or not we would once again be able to relax for a bit and eventually see our lives return to some semblance of how it used to be. The stress had taken a toll on both of us and yet I stood strong in my belief that our love could withstand it all as long as we were together. In fact, I was sure of it.

The night he came home and told me he was leaving turned my world upside down. He said he was no longer happy in our marriage and he wanted to separate. He kept telling me that I had spent too much time caring for sick family members and had failed to keep my focus on "us"; that he could no longer live with the disappointment of our lives being put on hold while everyone else's needs were being met. He said for years now he had been trying to tell me that I needed to stop giving so much of myself away, always tending to the needs of others instead of keeping my priorities straight. He told me that our life together should have been my first priority.

I tried to tell him that from the moment our life began, he became, and would always remain, my most precious love. I told him that my love for him was deep and pure. When I said I would do whatever it took to make things right he became angry and rebuked my words, suggesting that I was only trying to deflect my responsibilities for how I had failed him. He said he had tried a hundred times to tell me how he felt but I had refused to listen. No matter how many ways he tried to express his feelings to me, he said, I was deaf to his words.

I remember hearing the frustration in his voice when he reminded me of how I'd always told him that I knew him better than he knew himself. He said for a very long time he believed that to be true, until now. He told me it was clear to him that if I really knew him, the way I said I did, I should have recognized he felt as though I was putting his feelings and needs second place to everyone else in my life. He said he had tried to hold on and just accept his "lot" in life but it had become impossible for him. I could hardly believe what I was hearing. Maybe I didn't want to hear; maybe everything he was saying was true; maybe I had failed him as a wife and partner. His words were so sharp and cutting. With every sentence he spoke it felt as though he was slicing through my heart like a sharp knife cutting through hot butter. I knew there were occasions when he would get frustrated by the demands on my time but never for a moment did I think it would bring us to this point.

I questioned myself over and over again. How could I not have realized just how serious our problems had become? How could he feel as though I had let him down and hurt him so deeply when I felt he was the most important person in my life? How could he walk away from all of our hopes and dreams? How could he give up on us without a fight? I began to wonder if perhaps my commitment to him and the beautiful union we shared was more a part of my imagination than reality. Perhaps he never really loved me the way I loved him? Perhaps he wasn't the strong enduring man I believed him to be? Perhaps, perhaps, perhaps, what did it matter, he was gone and he wasn't coming home again.

❤

As I look back now I can see where little problems started to erupt. I struggled trying to make sense of it all. I kept asking myself, "Why us? Why me? Why now?" None of our problems seemed big enough or serious enough to cause this kind of marital collapse. I couldn't see it. I didn't sense it coming. Maybe I just hadn't wanted to see it or sense it. I was confused, wounded, and heartbroken. I felt like I was on a roller coaster ride and couldn't get off. I felt empty and alone.

It seems so strange now to think about how you can live through months of unhappiness and still believe in your heart that things will level out and your joy-filled life will return. I suppose it's what we all hope for in our marriages; a partner who loves and cares for us more than any one else in this world; a partner who is willing to stand by us, no matter what the circumstance. A partner is more than just your mate, a very best friend, a confidant, a lover, a protector; he is someone who knows your faults but loves you in spite of them. You know you can always count on a partner; someone who would never leave you simply because they love you too much. For the longest time I truly believed that was the kind of man I married. When I discovered I was wrong the pain of that realization was overwhelming.

I can't even begin to count the number of times I jokingly told my husband how frequently I had to pinch myself just to make sure this was really me and this was really my life. He would laugh and say, "Oh honey, this is your life, this is our life, and I love you." With everything in me I believed that to be true. I believed that ours was a life worth living. I believed our marriage was sacred and blessed. We had been married long enough to see our children grown, four work promotions for him, and an early retirement for me. We had stood together through the deaths of all four of our parents, the birth of our six grandchildren and finally, after years of searching for just the right place, a beautiful piece of property for the construction of our new home.

Our home was built on almost three acres of land. It has a spectacular rustic view of the mountains that dip into a magnificent jagged-rocked canyon filled with rich hues of blacks and grays interspersed with the red tinges of terra-cotta soil. It was a piece of Heaven that we found together and we rejoiced every day in the blessings that God had brought to us as we continued to build on our dreams.

We had worked four hard years developing our home and acreage into a park-like setting. We planted hundreds of colorful trees, shrubs and flowers of all varieties. We developed a small grape vineyard at the entrance of the property; the arborvitaes hedged us in and gave a sense of privacy from the more open areas of the land beyond our home's edge. To think this all began with acres of rocky soil and a pile of uprooted apple trees to the splendid site it was today was amazing. We were proud to say we had done it all by ourselves.

I remember how excited we were the day we purchased our old 1948 Eight-End Ford tractor, some garden tools, borrowed a brush hog, a cultivator, and went to work. We began by clearing the ground of all the extra rocks, tilled the soil, put in underground sprinklers, built a fence around half the property and finally planted acres of grass. It was just the beginning but it truly was a labor of love. We literally worked from sun up until sundown. We would joke about the fact that by the time my husband was ready to retire, everything we had planted would be fully matured and the property would be as lovely as any well-maintained park. Our evenings and weekends were often spent working in our yard. We enjoyed seeing it all come together and worked hard to make sure everything was impeccably tailored and clean.

We knew that taking care of our beautiful home, having a breathe-taking view and manicured yard meant that one day, when we were ready, the property would sell itself. We looked forward to having enough income to comfortably travel and enjoy the rest of our lives growing old together. We both believed that the efforts we made now would be the benefits we would reap later. To us, it was all worth it. We were making our dreams come true.

I can still recall how frequently we would chat with anticipation about the time when we could rest from the business of raising a family, working too many hours and having too many responsibilities. We looked forward to being able to relax and selfishly enjoy our time with one-another. I had never known a love like I felt with him. He was so precious to me and I was grateful for every moment we shared together.

❤

I will never forget that final decisive evening when he came home and announced to me that our marriage "wasn't working for (him) any more" and he was "moving out." He never used the word divorce but he did say that our life together was "over." It wasn't until later that I learned he had betrayed me. It took me a long time to realize that his leaving, or choosing not to work on resolving our marital problems, wasn't really about my lack of attention to his needs, as much as it was about his decision to search out things he had never experienced before in his life. He decided he wanted a different kind of life. I would never have believed it to be true had I not directly learned of it for myself. Saying I was devastated would be an understatement – the word destroyed comes to mind.

After that awful night I found myself feeling lost, alone and really just "existing." I felt numb and deserted. A couple of months before he left I was fortunate to find a part time job. I kept our home clean, took care of my two dogs and kept busy working in our yard, but the life I knew was gone and I wasn't accepting it very well. I was left trying to find a way to fight back from days of despair; spending most of my time feeling like someone had shot a hot cattle prod through my gut, while trying to remember if I had unplugged my curling iron or turned the outside water off.

There were many days that I just wanted to give up but somehow I didn't; I kept going. So many nights I would go to bed and pray that God would just take me home only to awaken a few hours later and realize that His answer was no, that wasn't His plan for my life.

There were days that I didn't want to clean house, do laundry, pay bills, go grocery shopping or even work in the yard. Most days it took every ounce of strength I had just to get out of bed. I made a habit of setting the wake-up button on my alarm clock and letting the buzzer sound until I could no longer bear the noise, forcing myself to get up and move. I didn't want to move. I couldn't seem to keep focused on any one task for more than a few minutes at a time. In many ways my grief had paralyzed me and I wasn't thinking clearly. I would write "to do" lists only to lose them or crinkle them up and throw them away because I didn't want to have to deal with one more "to do" that day. There were times I wanted to scream but mostly I cried.

Deep periods of loneliness consumed me. The anxiety was indescribable. I just knew I was going to spend the rest of my life in solitary confinement. I imagined myself as this little wrinkled old lady sitting in her rocking chair, looking out her window with nothing surrounding her but her emptiness. Life was going on "out there" for everyone else but life had nothing more to offer me. I had my life-partner, my soul mate, and now he was gone. "God help me," I thought. He took all that I held most precious in this life the day he walked out the door and this barrenness crept in.

❤

As I kept my eyes focused on the road, watching for my friend's truck to come whipping down the lane, the words I had spoken so many times to myself kept echoing over and over again in my head. "Pathetic," I'd think. "What a pathetic excuse for a human being you've become. You used to be fun, happy, filled with life – now look at you – you've lost fifty-eight pounds, your skin looks pallor and your hair has no life to it. You mope around, cry all of the time and bore your family and friends with the repeated cries of 'Why me?' 'I can't go on.' 'How do I survive?' 'How could this happen to me?' Pathetic, just pathetic," I told myself. Where was that strong Christian woman I had once been? How could my heart be broken this deeply? Where was my faith in the Lord? I then spoke aloud, "Where is my faith?"

❤

A moment later my thoughts were interrupted as I noticed my friend's big shiny black truck pulling into my driveway. As I opened the front door she looked towards me with that mischievously pleasing grin of hers. I watched as she lifted a hanger from the overhead door handle on the passenger's side of the truck. It was draped with a long white plastic bag. Written on the bag's front, in deep black lettering were the words, "Bon Marche." As she turned sideways in her seat, readying to exit the vehicle, she grabbed for the plastic bag and neatly folded it over her left arm. Once the bag was in place she reached back towards the passenger's seat again and picked up three small boxes. I curiously observed her movements as she gently set the boxes, one on top of the other, placing all three atop the plastic bag that was draped across her arm. I couldn't imagine what she was up to but continued to inquisitively observe her every movement as she carefully steadied the boxes with her right hand while exiting her truck, shutting the door with a snap of the back of her foot.

All smiles she came bouncing up the steps of my front porch and briskly announced, "Come on honey, we're headed to the bedroom." Without missing a beat she walked into my room. I followed her, wondering what in the world was going on. I observed her place the three small boxes neatly side by side on my bed. She took the hanger with the long plastic cover and very carefully removed the contents from the bag, exposing a gorgeous little black dress. "Isn't this wonderful?" she said, "Absolutely stunning isn't it?" "Yes, it's lovely," I replied. "Well honey, don't just stand there, get those clothes of yours off and put this dress on!" She motioned with a wave of her hand for me to start undressing.

With that little giggle of hers she continued, "You won't believe it but I bought that dress at a yard sale ten years ago for ten bucks! It looks like a Paris original, something Audrey Hepburn would have worn, don't you think?" I stood motionless looking at that beautiful black dress and then nodded my head in agreement. "The dress was so petite and looked so tiny. It would take someone very thin to look good in a style like that," I thought.

As I accepted the dress from my friend's hands I looked more closely at the style and feel of the dress' material. It was soft with just a touch of glimmer to its deep rich black color. She was right; the dress did remind me of something you would have seen in a famous 1950's movie. It was almost identical to the dress Audrey Hepburn wore when she starred with George Peppard in "Breakfast at Tiffany's." Knowing my friend's penchant for finding amazing items at yard sales I wouldn't have been a bit surprised if this wasn't a one-of-kind Paris original.

The top of the dress was scooped low in front with a kind of half-moon rounded curve across the décolletage. It had narrow shoulder straps. The back of the dress dropped down just past the shoulder blades into a v-shaped style. The bodice fit narrowly through the waist and hips then flared slightly as it captured three small ruffles, one flowing on top of the other, ending just above the ankle.

Distracted by my observations of the dress I heard my friend say, "Put it on, honey, and turn around." She smiled and nodded her head towards me as if encouraging me to put on the dress. I obeyed her direction like a small child following the leadings of her mother. "This dress brought me out of a real bad slump," she continued. "I've been where you've been, honey. I have felt that pain you're going through right now. I know what it's like to feel lonely, unworthy, totally unlovable – it's just awful, isn't it?"

I remained silent but couldn't help but wonder how she was so aware of exactly what was going on inside of me? I couldn't imagine anyone else experiencing the kind of intense pain that I was feeling, the kind that takes your breath away and makes your heart ache all of the time; the kind of pain you get through minute by minute because it hurts too much to think about surviving any longer than that. You dread nightfall because it encapsulates you with an overwhelming sense of isolation and solitude. You struggle with morning because it means you have to face another day alone. How could she really know how that felt? She was all smiles, chattering away and laughing as she spoke. She had so much energy and seemed so positive in her attitude. I didn't feel like that. I felt numb and sorrowful most of the time. I wondered to myself if she really knew what it was like to love someone with the intensity that I had loved the man who left me.

Lost in my thoughts I heard her say, "I wore this dress to a formal dance that I didn't really want to go to but my friend insisted. It was a fabulous event, a black tie and formal affair, 'A Warm Evening In September.' Doesn't that sound beautiful?" She chided. "It seems that I just came to a point when I knew it was time to start living again. I didn't plan it, it just happened. It took such a long time to move on, over a year I would guess. I didn't want to accept the invitation but my friend refused to take 'no' for an answer. She told me I just needed to get myself out of the house and away from the emptiness. I knew she was right but I still resisted. I loved that guy so much that I was willing to let myself shrink away and die for him." As I listened I thought to myself how much I would have felt just like her. I wouldn't have wanted to go to the dance either and I wondered if anyone could have convinced me the way her friend convinced her. At that moment I didn't think so.

She continued, "Now I realize how senseless my thinking was, destroying my life for him wasn't demonstrating some great love for him, it was simply giving up on me. I gave up the person I had been and I had no idea where my life was heading. I had no idea who the woman was that had taken up residency in my body. Everything felt so alien to me. I felt as if I had nothing to offer anyone, no value, no beauty, forget about self-worth or self-esteem – the mere thought of those words made me even more depressed."

"I can tell you this," she continued, "God never intended for that man, or any man for that matter, to become an Idol to me. But that is exactly what I had done. I had made this guy my Idol, sacrificing myself at his altar. He became like an addiction to me; my drug of choice if you will." She went on, "The Scriptures are pretty clear about the fact that we serve a jealous God. I think it's in Exodus 34 when the Lord tells Moses, 'Do not worship any other god, for the Lord, whose name is Jealous, is a jealous God.' Being a jealous God means the Lord is vigilant in guarding and watching over us. He is faithful, protective, and shielding. We serve an awesome God my friend and He has no desire for us to suffer in the dark places our mind takes us when we feel lost, rejected and alone. Fortunately, the Lord waits patiently for us to turn our thoughts and needs towards Him. The Lord knows the desires of our heart, that means He know the desires of your heart too, dear." She smiled and patted my face. "Jesus came to give us life and give it more abundantly. What man other than Jesus could do that for us," she questioned? She went on, "In return, He only asks that we believe in Him, a simple act of faith can turn your world around. His Word promises that gift to anyone who puts their trust in Him. The Lord's Word is truth, honey, you just can't see it or feel it right now but you will again. I promise you, you will."

I looked into the eyes of my friend and could see the earnestness of her words – it was obvious that she felt every word she spoke deep within her own heart. In my heart I also knew they were words filled with truth and hope. She was right; I was struggling to accept them as words of truth for me. It just hurt too badly right now, I thought.

Since I was a little girl and invited the Lord into my life I knew Jesus was real and He loved me. Now, He seemed so far away, so unreachable. I had enough faith to know that the Lord was watching over me but I wasn't convinced He was hearing neither my cries for help nor my pleas to be set free from the hurt.

As I listened to my friend I kept thinking how badly I wanted to believe that Jesus could turn my upside down world right side up again. I wanted to be like my friend. I wanted to put my focus somewhere other than on myself. I wanted to smile and laugh again like she was smiling and laughing. I wanted to be able to give tender words of encouragement or reach out to someone with a kind gesture of support like she was doing for me right now. Instead, I felt hopeless and helpless. I said a silent prayer, "Jesus, please help me to remember that the joy of the Lord is my strength and let the truth of my friend's words sink deep into my spirit."

Catching me a bit off guard my friend stated, "For a time I was so wrapped up in my worldly relationship with this man I had put God's love aside and sought the love of a human being over the love of our Heavenly Father. I heard someone say once that, 'God is closer to us than our own breath.' I'd say that's pretty close, wouldn't you?" She smiled at me again and without missing a beat continued, "Then I remembered I had this dress and my mother's formal evening gloves so I decided to doll up and go out. I figured even if I didn't have the greatest time of my life at least I would be around people and I'd get a good meal out of the deal." She laughed, "I wasn't eating much in those days. I lost forty pounds in three months, can you imagine? I loved being skinny but that wasn't the way to lose it; losing that much weight that fast really affected my health. God says we're the temple of the Holy Spirit and I became disgusted with the way I was caring for myself." Her words resonated in my mind as I thought of how woefully I had been caring for my own health.

She turned her back to me and was busying herself with the boxes she had placed on my bed as she continued to recount that awful, painful time in her life. I was intently listening to her when I noticed she was opening one of the three small boxes. "I spent hours getting ready," she went on, "which was good because it kept my mind occupied a smidgen. Of course, I was thinking about the guy who broke my heart the whole time, but I was also thinking about proving to myself that I could live my life without him. I've discovered I have a real stubborn streak." She mused. "I had to open my mind to the possibilities of life being good without him and let the Lord do the rest. Well girl, let me tell you, I not only went to that dance but I was the Belle of the ball! I felt like a million bucks! It must have shown because I literally danced the night away." I smiled at the thought of my friend finding happiness at such a dismal time in her life. It brought me a sense of comfort to hear that she found a way to overcome her feelings of despair. I was glad to see the joy in her. She deserved to be happy.

My friend paused for a moment as she pulled a pair of long white cotton gloves from one of the three little boxes. They were lovely too; definitely something Audrey Hepburn would have worn. Without saying a word she began to slide one of the gloves onto my hand and up my arm. The long white gloves ran all the way up my arms, just past the elbow. They had beautiful tiny pearl buttons that ran along the sides of my wrists. I stood there looking at her; still in awe of everything she was saying and unsure of where this experience was taking me. In truth, where we were headed didn't really matter to me, it was just so nice to have a moment of distraction. Being alone consumed me at times, so having her here, even if only for a brief moment, felt good to me. It gave me a small sense of emotional relief. Relief of any kind was a rarity these days. Besides, I was enjoying all of the attention. She winked at me as she witnessed my sheepish grin while watching her pull the second glove into place. I could feel my cheeks flush red although I don't know if she ever noticed.

"Turn around," she directed as she tugged on my shoulders until I was facing her. "Gorgeous!" she exclaimed. She turned back towards the bed, opened the second box and withdrew a beautiful pair of baguette diamond earrings. She handed them to me and motioned for me to put them on. "My son gave those to me," she stated as she reached for the contents of the third box. "I just love them. Go ahead, honey, put them on, they're even prettier on."

I continued to dutifully follow her every direction, amused by all the attention, and enjoying the excitement in her voice. My friend patiently waited as I put on her beautiful earrings. When I was finished she reached into the third box and picked up the most astonishing diamond necklace. It was more like a choker but it had baguette diamonds that matched the earrings perfectly.

"There." She stated emphatically, fastening the diamond choker around my neck. She took a short step backwards, stepping away from me as if she needed another perspective before giving me her final approval. The attentiveness of the look on her face was like that of someone who had just finished putting the final touches on a project they had been working on for months. "After all, she is an artist and has an incredible eye for detail," I thought.

"Look back this way," she directed as she extended her arms and gently turned me towards her again. She fussed with my hair for a moment or two, muttering under her breathe, audibly giving directions to her self on how my hair should be styled in order to match the rest of the look she was perfecting. She straightened the necklace she had so proudly placed around my neck, stepped back once more and smiled. I thought of the Scripture in Malachi 3 that says we are like a jewel in God's eye. I didn't feel much like a jewel but my friend was certainly giving her best efforts to make me feel that way. I just kept thinking how incredibly kind she was treating me.

I couldn't help but wonder how she came up with the idea of doing this for me in the first place. Awkwardly I asked, "What exactly are we doing?" She responded with a laugh, "Playing dress up, honey; we're just playing dress up." "Dress up? Why are we playing dress up?" I queried to myself. Truthfully, the reason for that didn't really matter either. What mattered was this precious woman had taken time to come to my home with the sole purpose of doing something special for me. She came just to let me know I was not alone. Someone understood. Someone cared. Someone really, really cared. "How thoughtful is that?" I pondered.

As I fixed my eyes on her every move I was trying to remember where in the Scriptures the verse was of how a friend sticks closer than a brother. "I'd have to look that one up after she left", I decided. She had no idea of the thoughts and feelings that were running through my mind as I was basking in all of her attentive care. If she did know, she never let on, but continued to busy herself with each step of her intended design.

I had no idea what the dress must have looked like on me. I felt more like a bystander watching an artist create a picture from a blank canvas, anxious to see her final masterpiece. As she continued to fuss, straighten and rework my hairstyle I thought perhaps she felt more like a dress designer who was creating an impeccable appearance for a mannequin in a department store display window. In my mind's eye I saw a very kind person reaching out to touch the heart of a hurting friend. Watching her concentrate on every detail of my "new look" brought a slight smile to my face. I could never have put into words how it was moving my heart.

As I obediently continued to respond to her every command, I couldn't help but think of how amazing it was that she could have gone through something as painful as I was going through and yet she was smiling, laughing, and focused on me instead of herself. I had been so self-absorbed in my loss that I didn't have time for anything more than my daily pity party. Now here was this beautiful woman, wonderful friend, standing at the side of my bed dressing me in her favorite dress and finest jewels. It made me feel a little ashamed of how pitiful I'd become.

"Grief does strange things to us," I reasoned. "Maybe my husband had become an Idol to me too? Maybe he had been my 'drug of choice' as my friend had described? Maybe God sent her to tell me this isn't the life He ever intended for me?"

In Jeremiah 29:11 it says, "For I know the plans I have for you, declares the Lord, plans to prosper you and not to harm you, plans to give you hope and a future." Maybe sending this friend to my door was His way of reminding me that although I wanted to give up on myself, He wasn't giving up on me. I felt comforted by the thought.

As my friend continued to busy herself, Scriptures began flooding through my mind. Proverbs 18:10, "The name of the Lord is a strong tower; the righteous run to it and are safe." Psalm 28:7, "The Lord is my strength and my shield; my heart trusts in him, and I am helped. My heart leaps for joy and I will give thanks to him in song." In Psalms 56:8 the Word says, "You keep track of all my sorrows. You have collected all my tears in a bottle. You have recorded each one in your book." I silently prayed. "Oh Lord, you must have an ocean full of bottles for me. Please forgive my weaknesses and let me once again stand strong in your Word."

❤

My friend said she had come to play dress up with me. What a tender way to help a women whose heart is broken, I thought. I had long past forgotten my childhood days of playing dress up and yet in that moment I felt like a little girl again. I felt that sense of uncertainty, anticipation and excitement about how I might look in this lovely dress. I wanted to feel pretty. I wanted to feel something good about myself. I wanted to feel as my friend did, like the Belle of the ball but I wasn't sure I knew how. I just didn't see myself that way. I saw a sad, lonely, miserable woman but my dear friend saw possibilities in me that I couldn't see in myself. I didn't know how or why but I was glad that she did. There was hope in the thought.

It appeared as though my friend was nearing the end of her "dress up" endeavor when I saw her look up at me and smile with a big grin. She slowly began to move; walking around me as she painstakingly reviewed every inch of my new look from head to toe. She carefully checked every detail as she moved. It was so sweet to see how much enjoyment my friend was deriving from her labors. It was as though, for a moment, she was allowing me to enter into her childhood joy of playing dress up whenever she needed to feel comforted or encouraged in her own life.

I remember her telling me about all of the times she would secret herself away in her mother's large closet and surround herself with the many beautiful evening gowns her mother owned. She told me of how she would pretend to be a beautiful princess readying herself for her prince charming. She said she would try on many of the lovely formals that hung on their satin hangers just waiting for her choosing. She would imagine her first appearance at the ball and how astounded everyone would be at how beautiful she looked. She said that she loved those beautiful formals, the delicateness of the fabrics; the soft feel of the taffetas and silks. She recalled how she would stand and look at herself in the mirror and how she would twist and sway so she could see the sparkle of the lovely pearls, sequins and other bright colored gems that adorned the dresses. She said that her mother was a very attractive woman so when she would slip on one of her dresses she felt beautiful too. She felt like the treasure every woman dreams and desires to be.

My thoughts turned to my friend and the pain she had been through in the loss of her relationship. I so admired her honesty. I wondered how anyone could have ever hurt her. How could anyone have ever given her up? She is so giving and I am so blessed to have her in my life. She has supported me in too many ways to even count and here she is again, finding another way to reach out to me and tell me, 'you matter; you're okay; you'll make it through this; I believe in you, believe in yourself.' Women who share a true friendship are given such a special gift; a cherished blessing that God sends as a reminder of His great love and compassion for us. At that very moment I decided that I needed to find a way to tell her how much her friendship means to me. However, I realized that I was just too filled with emotion right now to even speak. "But I will," I thought, "Someday I will let her know just how special she has made me feel and how much I value her in my life."

So many different thoughts and feelings were whirling around in my head as my friend proceeded to put the final touches on her new creation. "I don't even know the man's name that broke her heart and I'm angry at him," I said to myself. I wasn't just angry because he hurt my friend so deeply but because he was so foolish to give up such an extraordinary woman like her in the first place. "Some men have a lot to learn," I decided.

❤

My thoughts were abruptly interrupted again when she took my face in her hands and stated, "Okay, honey, we're ready. Turn around, step up and look into that mirror." With those words she tenderly turned me towards the large mirror that hung from an antique dresser my husband and I had purchased on our tenth wedding anniversary. I turned towards the mirror as instructed. I felt almost hesitant to look up. "Look!" she exclaimed, "Look at that beautiful woman in the mirror!" Feeling somewhat embarrassed, and a bit shy, I looked up and into the mirror. As my eyes came into focus with my image I felt hesitant to respond, it was as if my mind refused to accept the fact that the person I was looking at in the mirror was me. Without thinking I softly replied, "Yes, it is a beautiful dress." Almost defiantly my friend stepped in front of me and responded, "No, that's not what I said! I said look at that beautiful woman in the mirror!"

As she repeated her words she ever so slightly placed her hands on the sides of my face and turned my head toward her, looking directly into my eyes. "I want you to listen to me very carefully my dear friend. God created a real beauty when He made you. You are a beautiful woman, on the inside and out. Any man who would give you up is a fool because he is losing a treasure. You are a treasure and you need to recognize that about yourself." She turned me back towards the mirror and repeated her words for a third time, "See, just look at that beautiful woman in the mirror!" The tears welled in my eyes. I couldn't speak. I couldn't tell her how her act of love had moved me beyond words. I felt confused, unsure and grateful all at the same time.

I turned and stared at my image in the mirror again. "She really is thin," I thought, "a lot thinner than I realized." As I studied my reflection I found myself resisting the idea that the woman in the little black dress was me. It was the first time that I truly recognized how much my physical appearance had changed over the past several months. I stared blankly for a moment as I tried to absorb the changes I was seeing.

In my peripheral vision I noticed my friend standing at the side of my antique dresser watching me. She had her arms crossed in front of her; her head was tilted slightly to her left side. I turned and glanced at her without saying a word but

I was sure the look in my eyes betrayed my thoughts. She grinned at me and nodded her head affirmatively. Her smile was a silent expression of encouragement. I felt a blush of confidence flood over me as I turned to look into the mirror once again. My mind was conflicted, "That really is me," I thought. "My dear friend wants me to see myself from a different perspective. She wants me to see my potential instead of my failure. She wants me to see promise instead of defeat. I want to see it too," I reasoned. "Oh, Lord," I prayed, "I really want to see it too."

In actuality, what I saw was how horribly I was struggling with the way my life was now. I had lost my sense of "self" and I felt as though I no longer held an identity. I knew who I used to be but I had no idea who I was supposed to be. In that moment I realized if there is life after losing the man I believed held all my future hopes and dreams, this gesture of love was certainly a way to show me that truth. It definitely gave me pause; something to really think about.

❤

Stepping in front of me and blocking my view in the mirror she placed her hands on the sides of my face again. My friend spoke, "I love you, honey. Lots of people love you." She went on, "You have blessed my life. You are very special to me, just like you are special to so many other friends who care about you and want to help you through this terribly difficult time. Don't ever forget that God loves you too, more than anyone else ever could. He wants the very best for you. He wants your focus to be on Him and the plans He has for your life."

Taking my shoulders in her hands she studied my face. I could see the tears forming in her eyes. Ever so gently she whispered, "I love you, dear friend. I truly love you." She hesitated for a moment, blinked her eyes, and then with the slightest of grins she teasingly stated, "Now, take off my little black dress."

Without another word she stepped behind me and unzipped the back of that beautiful black dress. As I slipped it off my shoulders and handed it to her she smiled and said, "We're going to have to make you your own little black dress, honey." I smiled slightly but remained without words. How do you express in words something the heart feels so deeply that it leaves you speechless? How do you tell someone that their act of kindness has given you a bridge to healing that you never expected or thought possible? How do you ever convey your thoughts or emotions in a way that truly communicates the feelings held deep within your soul?

God's timing is perfect, I observed. He knew how much I needed someone to physically reach out and allow me to feel His presence. God knew; He always knows exactly what we need and exactly when we need it.

❤

I watched as my friend quickly packed up the three small boxes and slid the black dress back under the plastic cover and out of sight. I stood there, still, without words, but in my heart I knew she knew that her kind deed had gone beyond the gift of language. It was an act of love, a charitable endowment that went further than the boundaries one could convey with any spoken word. I knew she understood my heart though no utterance would form in my mouth. The Scripture from Psalms 46:10 came to my mind, "Be still and know that I am God." I realized that sometimes in the stillness of a moment more feelings are expressed than any words could ever articulate.

I continued to observe as she carefully packed away the final box of her small treasures; gently tucking each one carefully back into its own container. When she was finished she turned and smiled at me. We walked silently to my front door. As she stepped through the doorway she turned and smiled at me again. "Remember, I love you, honey." I anxiously replied, "I love you too, Janet – more than you'll ever know." The words barely eked from my throat. She wrapped her arms around me and hugged me tightly to her chest. "Oh honey, honey, honey," she softly whispered in my ear, "You're going to be okay, you really will." With that she turned and headed back towards that big black shiny truck of hers.

I watched as she re-hung the plastic bag on the passenger's side front window. She placed the three small boxes in the seat next to the bag and closed her truck door. As she pulled out of the driveway she smiled again, waving goodbye. Fighting to hold back my tears I attempted a smile and waved back towards her. I watched until her truck was completely gone from my sight. She left as quickly as she had arrived. Quietly I spoke, "Thank you Janet. You have no idea how God just used you to touch my life."

❤

As I walked back through the doorway and into the stillness of my empty home I felt her presence. "God truly does always send the very best. His timing truly is perfect," I reflected. I stood there silently and relived the moment we had just experienced together.

Slowly, I made my way back to my bedroom, looking at the empty bed where once her gifts of loving kindness had laid. I turned and looked into the antique mirror. I closed my eyes and envisioned the woman I had just witnessed moments before standing in front of that mirror in that beautiful black dress.

As the image of that woman took focus in my mind I allowed all of the words of my friend to filter through my thoughts again. "You are a beautiful woman. Any man who thinks he doesn't want you is a fool. You are a treasure, a true gift. God has something very special in store for you, my friend, but you need to change the dance. Your steps need to be in step with your Heavenly Father. You need to follow His lead for your life. You need to reclaim the life God has intended for you. You need to take back control of what is rightfully yours – you have the right to be happy, you have the right to enjoy God's blessings and you have the right to be all that the Lord intended for you to be. Remember dear friend, God's word says that His promises are from everlasting to everlasting. He has a purpose for your life beyond anything you ever imagined. He gave you your heart, your wisdom, your beauty and your loving spirit. He knows the pain in your heart right now, honey. There's nothing we can suffer that Christ has not already suffered - and so much more."

I imagined Janet reaching forward and patting my face again, her words resonated through my mind. "God loves you, honey, He really loves you. He's closer to you than your own breath." As I recounted her words I was reminded of a song that the contemporary Christian artist, Crystal Lewis sings based on Isaiah 61 Verse 3; "He gives beauty for ashes, strength for fear, gladness for mourning, and peace for despair." "How true," I thought. Even when we feel like we're wearing the weight of the world on our shoulders, like we're surrounded with nothing but loss and grief, the Lord is there tenderly reminding us that He is with us – He will never leave us or forsake us.

As I continued to sift through Janet's words to me I thought about what she had said to me about faith. "If you believe, all it takes is a simple act of faith. God can dramatically change our lives with a simple act of faith." "Oh Lord, I prayed, increase my faith, please increase my faith."

❤

The next day while shopping at a local department store I walked past the card section and noticed a plain white card with a little black dress on the front of it. The outside of the card read, "Every woman needs one perfect little black dress and one friend she can talk to about anything." The inside of the card read, "I'm still looking for that dress." I picked up the card and spoke a quick prayer. "Thank you Lord. Thank you for showing me the ideal card to send to my friend. It's wonderful. It's perfect. Just perfect!

As I made my way to the check out stand to purchase the card I couldn't help but think how interesting it was that I had noticed this one card amidst the hundreds that were stacked around it. There it was; one single card with a little black dress on the cover and the perfect quote for my friend. "That's the definition of a coincidence," I thought, "A minor miracle in which God chooses to remain anonymous." I was sure God had placed that card in just the right spot, exactly where I'd be sure and find it. I couldn't wait to give it to her.

♥

A few days later I found myself in the sanctuary of my church. As I knelt down at the foot of the cross of Jesus I began to sob uncontrollably. "Lord," I began, "I'm here because I need to confess to you how the pain of losing the life I once knew crushed me, and it crushed my spirit. It hurt me so deeply, Lord, that I lost sight of You. Forgive me, Jesus, that I allowed the love of a man to become more important in my life than my love for You. Right now Lord, I willingly surrender my husband, my marriage and my life to You. I lay all of the loss, the hurt and the pain at Your feet dear Jesus. Forgive me Lord for the ways in which I have failed; cleanse me and wash me with Your love." "Lord," I wept, "I receive whatever plan You have for my life. I ask You to fill me, teach me, use me, do with me whatever is pleasing to You dear Jesus."

"And Lord," I continued, "Thank You for sending me so many wonderful friends who have stood by me, listened to me, wept with me and prayed for me. I pray a special blessing upon each and every one of them. May You bring an extra portion of joy to my dear friend Janet who encouraged me with Your Word and so compassionately demonstrated Your love to me in a very tangible way. Thank You Lord. Thank You," I cried.

♥

Of the many lessons I've learned in life, I now know one thing for sure - Jesus is a wound healer. In Psalms 147:3 the Word tells us that He heals the brokenhearted and binds up their wounds. God truly never gives up on us. He is always there, patiently waiting for us to come back to His loving arms. He answers our prayers. His desire is to heal our hearts and to bring us closer to Him. When we hurt, Jesus hurts. When we suffer, Jesus suffers. When we open our hearts to Him, Jesus is ready and willing to heal us and bring us back to a rightful relationship with Him.

In the book of Jude, verse 21, the Lord tells us to never go outside the boundaries of where His love can reach us. I realized I had stepped outside that boundary for a while. I lost my way and my faith was on shaky ground. For a time I feared I would never find my way back. My faith had become so weak but very slowly I began to see how in Christ our weaknesses can be made whole and strong again. I knew it would be a long road but there was no where else I wanted to be. I wanted God's healing grace. I wanted to renew my strength and I wanted to feel good and at peace again.

❤

As I prepared to leave the church sanctuary I picked up my Bible and noted a quote I had written several years ago on the inside cover. It simply read, "There were times when I have questioned the presence of God in my life, fortunately He has never questioned His presence in mine." I thought for a long time about that quote. I had not written it at a time I was questioning my faith. I was not struggling with any heartache or misery in my life. I remember writing the quote when a dear friend of mine was struggling with the break up of her marriage. As I was praying for her those words came to my mind so I wrote them on the inside cover of my Bible. I ran my fingers over the words I had written. I had never imagined the words would someday also be written for me. "There it is again, Lord, another confirmation of your faithfulness." I affirmed. "Your Word says that in You, Lord, I am valued and have worth; through You, Jesus, there is meaning and purpose for my life. Perhaps most importantly,

I have the loving gift of Your Holy Spirit dwelling within me, desiring to use me for God's glory. How could anyone find more value in living than that? I may have lost the sense of Your presence in my life for a time but how gracious You are Lord to never lose Your sense of presence in mine."

As I walked outside the church doors and into the fresh afternoon air I closed my eyes, took a very deep breath and allowed the warmth of the afternoon sun to flood over my face. "One last thing Lord, thank You for never giving up on me. Thank You for patiently waiting for me. I will never leave Your loving arms again," I vowed.

"And Lord," I hesitated, "thank You for affectionately reminding me of who I am in You, through the kindheartedness of a true friend with a little black dress." Amen. ❤

"Do not withhold Your mercy from me, LORD;
may Your love and faithfulness always protect me."
Psalm 40:11
NIV

The Little Black Dress Party

Originally, "The Little Black Dress" story was written as a gift for my friend, Janet. I wanted to commit to writing the memory of the day she arrived at my front door with her little black dress in hand. I wanted to find a special way to thank her for how beautifully she demonstrated her love and support towards me during such a very difficult and painful time in my life. I wanted the two of us to be able to look back twenty years from now and joyfully reflect on that precious moment when our very extraordinary friendship took root and began to grow.

I knew I wasn't a professional writer so I didn't expect the text to be perfect. I didn't expect perfect at all. I simply wanted the words to convey my appreciation for how deeply Janet blessed my life with her vibrant act of love. I wanted her to always remember that her desire to help me feel better by "playing dress-up with me" actually drew me into a closer relationship with the Lord.

Janet reminded me that when we think our lives are lost and our failures are posted on the giant billboards of life, for the whole world to see, there remains a place of refuge and healing. Our Heavenly Father is steadfast in His love for us. He feels our hurts. He understands our pain. He desires for us to reach for Him through His Word and He ministers to us through family, friends and our circumstances. He is faithful. He is real. He understands our wounds better than we do. He is, after all, our wound healer. He is greater than our pain. He is stronger than our loss and He can right any failure in our lives if we are willing to turn that loss over to Him.

I struggled for so long with the "turning it over" part. I didn't want to give up. I wanted my husband and my life back. I wanted things to be the way they used to be. I fought a war within myself that exhausted me and caused me to give up hope on more days than I care to count. I believed in Philippians 4:13, "I can do all things through Christ who strengthens me." I just wasn't ready to be strengthened. I knew the longer I fought surrendering my desires to the Lord the longer my recovery. Yet I still resisted. I just couldn't seem to force myself to let go of my dreams and give up on the way I wanted things to be. It seems I had forgotten the verse in Proverbs 16:3 that tells us to, "Commit to the Lord whatever you do, and your plans will succeed." I wanted the future that God had planned for me but I had not committed my plans to Him. I was desperate for His hope and I thought I was searching for a way to let go and lean into the promises of God. In reality, I fought letting go and I tried with everything in me to direct God's plan for my life *my* way.

Slowly, I began to realize that what I was really doing was searching for a way to convince God that my life should be restored and I should be allowed to have my abundant life the way I envisioned it to be. I worked hard at convincing myself that was the way it was supposed to be. I dreamed of the way I wanted things to be. I was so certain that my "knight in shining armor" was about to return home at any moment. Together, we would show the world that restoration and reconciliation was God's plan for us all along. I was even prepared to write another addendum to "The Little Black Dress." I was going to call it, "The Little Black Dress ~ Restored."

Do I sound desperate yet? I was. I was desperate to have my life turn out the way I wanted without any real thought or care about what God's plan might be for me. If I believed that God always has a better plan for us than we can create for ourselves, then why wasn't I earnestly willing to turn it all over to Him? Many times I contemplated that Scripture in Proverbs that directs us to commit our plan to the Lord and it will succeed. But I was only willing to commit to *my* plan - not His plan for me. No wonder I was having so much trouble succeeding in my recovery. I didn't submit anything to the Lord. I hung on to the hope of my life returning to how it was before, like a tigress would hold on to her newborn cub in the wilderness, I refused to give up. Nothing was going to take my belief in our marital reconciliation away from me – not even God's plan. I rejected anything that didn't fit my strategy for restoration because I believed that the only thing that would ever make me feel happy and whole again was the life I had before.

I worked hard at trying to make every Scripture I read fit my way of thinking. I tried to convince myself that the nightmare would end just as soon as my husband recognized what he had lost. Memories flooded over me daily and I just kept telling myself that those memories had to be flooding through his mind too. I just knew if I held on long enough he would eventually want to fight for our marriage as much as I did. On the other hand, I truly believed that the weight of healing my marriage was solely on my shoulders and God was calling me to "stand" and to "stand strong." I read as many Scriptures as I could find about what it meant to "stand." There are many. I wanted those Scriptures to fit my plan too.

The problem was I was willing to "stand" but I had no sense of how anything was going to change. I didn't have any direction as to how I was going to implement this transformation in our marriage or how I was going to convince my husband to participate. He came in and out of my life for months and months after we separated. I could see he was struggling with what had happened to us too. I believe at one time both of us knew what we had lost but neither of us had found a way to fix what was wrong. There was so much emotional turmoil and distress over the loss of trust, the sense of betrayal, the pain of the break-up that most of our conversations ended badly and we both felt worse than before. There were times when we saw a glimpse of hope that perhaps we could reconstruct our life only to see that hope dashed by another emotional let down. I do believe that broken marriages are repairable and that everyone should try but I've learned that it takes much more than just one partner wanting it to be so. As I look back now I can see I had no real plan. I just had a broken heart that wanted to be quickly mended and I believed that restoring my marriage was the way to do it. I think most would call that a plan for disaster. God's plan was not at the core of my desires and I had no foundation on which to "stand."

I wanted to pray but I didn't want to listen. I wanted to tell God how it was going to be instead of surrendering my needs to Him and allowing Him to direct my path. I wanted to reject the truth of what the Scriptures said and run in the other direction. I wanted God's Word to say what I wanted to hear but that wasn't happening.

How is it that one can lead them self to believe they have the power to change someone else by holding on for dear life to the things their heart tells them they need? Forget about whether or not it's healthy or good for you. You want it. You fight for it. You refuse to give up. I will say I was persistent, even stubborn, in what I believed was meant to be. During that time, no one could have convinced me that my marriage was not God's plan for my life. Now I often wonder how one gets things so emotionally turned around in their head that they think being faithful to their own desires is eventually going to make God see how right they are and that He should adjust His plan according to theirs. Sad isn't it, but I did that too.

I was finally able to recognize that what I was insisting on was not God's promise to me at all but instead my selfish concoction of how I thought my life should be. It was a relief when I gradually began to surrender. I remember literally cupping my hands and raising them toward Heaven in a physical act of surrender. It was then that I handed my loss, my fears, my sense of rejection, my low self-esteem and my weakened spirit up before the Lord.

I can still remember my prayer, "Lord, Your Word tells us that Your yoke is easy and Your burden is light. My burden is too much for me to bear any longer. I don't have the power or the strength to continue to fight this battle alone.

Please forgive me Lord for constantly taking my problems back and trying to fix myself on my own terms. Forgive me for my stubbornness and my unwillingness to listen. I give my burdens to you Lord. I place them in Your capable hands. I give them all to You and pray that You will give me the wisdom and strength to never try and take them back into my own hands again. If I have to surrender my loss and my needs to You every day, every minute, or every second of every day, let me do so Lord. I so very much want to surrender."

So often I had to remind myself of the promises of God and refuse to get in the way of His plan for my life. He knows the thoughts He has toward us and if we give ourselves to Him, Jesus will bring us a future where peace and promise exist. The key word is, "He." He knows the plans He has towards us. He knows the future that is best for us and He knows the promises He has given to us. It was the Lord who desires to fill me with good things, not me telling Him how it was to be done and then standing back and waiting for Him to magically make all things new according to "me".

In Psalm 37:23 the Word states, "The Lord directs the steps of the godly. He delights in every detail of their lives." I kept reading that verse, "The Lord directs the steps of the godly," not 'I' direct. "He delights in every detail of their lives." Yes, He delights in every detail of our lives when we allow Him to direct our steps. I wasn't allowing Him to direct my steps. I was asking Him to get in step with me. I was telling the God of the universe, the Creator of all things great and small that He needed to get in step with me. How inanely foolish and short-sided I was in my thinking. No wonder I fought and struggled for so long without any relief. I was fighting against the very One who was waiting to take me into His arms and whisper in His still, small voice, "I am here. I am the One you seek. I am your Wound Healer, your Deliverer and King. I am." Ouch.

❤

So on to the writing of "The Little Black Dress." Once I finished my story for Janet, I asked my friend Vonda if she would let me read the text to her before presenting my gift to Janet. As I read, Vonda closed her eyes and listened to what I had written. When I had finished the reading, I looked at Vonda to see tears streaming down her face. She said to me, "Oh Robyn, this story needs to go beyond a gift for Janet or a keepsake for you. It is a story about how women can love and support one another. It's a story about friendship. Putting that dress on you and reminding you of how valuable you are to others, but especially to the Lord, is something a lot of women need to hear - particularly women who are grieving over the loss of a relationship, or women who are experiencing feelings of insecurity and low self-esteem. We all know women who could benefit from this story and the unique way in which one woman encouraged another. I believe it needs to be shared."

As we talked, Vonda said that she had a group of women that she would like to invite for a reading of the book and I should invite some of my friends too. We talked about asking everyone that was invited to wear their favorite little black dress. We prayed over the story and then sent out invitations to a select group of woman asking them to join us for a potluck and book reading. That night, "The Little Black Dress Party" was born.

When the evening of the party finally arrived I remember feeling anxious and a bit nervous. It didn't take long before

I felt very comfortable and relaxed with this remarkable group of women – many of whom I was meeting for the first time. The evening began with us sharing a meal of several deliciously prepared foods - each woman brought their favorite main dish, salad or dessert. The food was delectable and as we dined together each woman moved around the room introducing themselves and chatting like old friends. It was amazing to me how warm and inviting each woman was to the others. We all felt so comfortable, as if we had known each other for years. I'm pretty sure God had His hand in our selection process.

Once we had completed our meal we all retreated to the formal living room for the reading of "The Little Black Dress." Vonda gave a brief introduction about the story. I remember looking at Janet while Vonda was explaining how the story was written for a dear friend of mine who did something extraordinary to help me through the troubled times since my separation. Janet was very quiet. I don't think at that point anyone had realized yet that the story was about her.

At the conclusion of the reading there was a quiet calm that fell over the room. No one spoke. It was as though each person was contemplating some of their own life struggles; each reflecting on their own personal losses; their own personal journey through their pain and eventually their recovery. Slowly, several of the women began to share their thoughts. Many spoke of painful moments in their lives, the loss of a love, the break up of a marriage, the loss of family, the hurt, the anger, the "why me" and the "why now."

One of the women commented to Janet, "My dear, how did you ever think to do something as unique as this? What you did had to be God inspired. It was done with such quiet elegance." In her demure way, Janet smiled and simply stated, "I just wanted Robyn to feel better about her self. When I was little, playing dress up always made me feel better and I wanted Robyn to feel better too." She was right. Janet came with that little black dress just to "play dress up" with me, in hopes of making me feel better about myself because she understood my pain. She understood my grief and that place of brokenness where I resided day after day.

In reality, Janet brought me so much more that evening than just a little black dress to play dress up. On that day she brought me my first step on a long bridge to healing. Her act of compassion sent me to my knees in prayer. The love and support I felt from her wrote the words to "The Little Black Dress ~Wounded Heart ~ Healing God," and the expression of that love grew into "The Little Black Dress Party."

It's like what the Lord tells us in Genesis 50:20, what the enemy would have for evil, God will have for good. God took the pain of my loss and sent a beautiful woman with a little black dress to my door. That act created a desire in me to write a book of thanks that resulted in another friend hearing about this charming gesture; believing it must go beyond a memory for me or a gift of thanks to a single friend. This prompted a book reading with a group of fabulous Christian women, all outfitted in their little black dresses, which then resulted in an addition to the little black dress story called, "The Little Black Dress Party."

The words you read here came from that sweet moment in time when one friend found a tender way to reach out to another friend in need. God took one small act of generosity, filled it with love and let it grow. In 1 Corinthians 3:6

Paul writes, "I Paul planted the seed, Apollos watered it but God made it grow." One must never underestimate God's plans for us or how He moves in our lives. Only through His mercy and grace did an innocent gift of love grow into moments of joy and healing from one to many.

❤

Before my life was turned upside down I was always the one who wanted to be the caregiver; the one who wanted to be the person others would feel comfortable coming to for love and support. When I was a teenager my mother used to tell me that she was sure that I would grow up to be the next generations, "Dear Abby." My professional life was much the same as my personal life. I worked in law enforcement, prosecution, victim services and participated in both a local and national crisis response team. I loved being the giver but I had never been very comfortable being on the receiving end. God used this experience to teach me a better way of thinking. He taught me that learning to reach out for help and accepting it is as much a gift as giving – maybe even more so.

As a result of my resistance to change I found myself on the receiving end of need for a very long time. I cried out to my family and my friends. I begged for their prayers. I sought solace and strength from the strong women who encompassed me; Godly women who knew the wounds of sorrow but also new the joy of victory in Jesus. These women encircled me with their love, compassion and kindness. They prayed with me. I prayed. Some read Scriptures to me. I searched the Scriptures – sometimes looking for answers but most of the time looking for words that would relieve the ache inside of me. I went to our churches Healing Room; I went to women's church groups. I spent time with

Christian friends who ministered the Word of the Lord to me. I had people from my church who were gifted in praying for others come and pray through my home. I took every opportunity to try and feel God's presence. I sought to break the emotional ties that kept me from moving forward. I wanted to stop fighting. I wanted to let go but something deep inside of me fought back and kept telling me to hold on. It was a tug of war inside of me and it nearly tore me apart.

If there were deeper words than broken and humbled, I would use them to describe me. I refused to accept the idea of getting better because it meant letting go. I resisted constructive criticism because it wasn't what I wanted to hear. I had an argument ready for every reason why I should let go and move on. And then one day I finally let go. I don't know why. I don't know how. I just know that I finally laid my wounds at the feet of Jesus and withdrew my hands. It felt scary but it felt good too. Mostly, it felt right. I knew I was beginning to find that illusive peace that I had sought for so long.

Recovery doesn't come over night. In fact I would say there are still days that I struggle with the twinges of loss but when I do I go to my Source. I go to the Scriptures. I read, study and pray. When ever I would find my feelings falling back into that dark hole of misery and abandonment I would once again dig my heels in and say, "Help me Lord, I refuse to go back to that dismal and lonely place. I do not belong in a sea of despair. I need to get my thinking straight. I cannot reason with my emotions. I must reason by the grace of God and the power of the Holy Spirit." As I prayed, that same familiar Scripture would resound in my mind, "The joy of the Lord is my strength." It really is true. While this Scripture has always held considerable meaning to me, it wasn't until my thinking became clearer that I discovered the true depth of its significance.

♥

During the little black dress party, as one woman began to share, so did another, then another and then another. Many gave examples of some very sorrowful moments in their lives. Some used humor while others recalled their sense of rejection, loss of hope and feelings of desolation with great emotion and intensity.

I wish I could put into words the magic of that evening. We listened to each other and encouraged one another with a nod, a smile or a comment. Everyone was engaged with each others feelings and showed an uncanny understanding of each others experiences. I believe there is an unspoken union when you share your grief with someone who has been there too; with someone who knows the hurt and has felt the agony of losing someone they deeply loved. It is a connection that cannot be explained in simple terms, or complicated terms for that matter. It is a sense, an unexplainable feeling, a knowing. It is real, pure and healing.

Eventually, the stories of grief began to flow into stories of triumph and restoration. Many spoke of how long it took to overcome their loss, how relationships ebb and flow and when a relationship ends, a part of you ends with it. They spoke about how there comes a moment in time when your broken heart begins to mend. How you don't always notice the healing right away but you slowly begin to see life from a new perspective. You begin to dare to believe in yourself again. You begin to feel little bits and pieces of your joy return. You begin to recognize that you are regaining control and moving forward with your life. You actually catch yourself smiling or laughing on occasion. At first you may feel a little guilty because you are so used to feeling sad and blue. Then you realize that God has not called you to a life of sorrowful depression and you learn to go ahead and smile a little bigger and a little more often too.

At first you can look back and count the moments during the day that your thoughts were about the one you lost and in those moments you are hit with waves of nausea or anxiety that is incomprehensible. Then, one day, you realize that time has past and that person hasn't been at the center of your universe for the entirety of your day. You actually discover moments of peace and tranquility that you had forgotten ever existed. You thank God for His quite presence, put your chin up, square your shoulders and move on.

Many of the women discussed how the memory of the loss never leaves you but the sting it produces diminishes. How the mind heals but the heart never forgets. We spoke of how you begin to believe that your life will go on, that it can be better, and you will have a life worth living again. We talked about how you discover that you can pray again and know that the Lord hears those prayers. You can feel the sun on your face and hear the laughter of people enjoying life around you and feel sincerely happy for them. You can smile too – a real smile, not one that is painted on like that of a circus clown – a real true, "I mean it" kind of smile. Eventually, you realize that there is hope on the other side of grief. You become determined to succeed.

The little black dress party truly was a magical evening of love and fellowship. On that night, a common bond of understanding was shared; a common bond of friendship was born. I believe that night we all grew in our appreciation for the beauty and strength found in a woman's spirit when her heart is founded in Christ. We shared our hearts that night. We shared our emotions in truth and we shared our love. ❤

Conclusion

Be encouraged, dear one, if you are reading this little book. It was shared with you because someone who loves you cares about what you are going through. They want you to know that you are loved and you are not alone. Many of us have been where you are right now. While it might not seem like life will ever get better, it will - know that this is true. I struggled for over four years before I found my way back to the throne of grace, but find it I did. I pray that your journey will not take as long as mine but if it does, remember that the Lord is walking you through. He surrounds you with His mercy, His love, His healing power and His grace. His desire is to draw you to Him and fill you to overflowing with His peace and His joy.

Close your eyes and allow the Lord's presence to surround you. Listen to His still, small voice. Pray and study the Word of the Lord. They are words of truth and healing. He will teach you everything you need to know about overcoming this sad and lonesome time in your life. He will renew your strength. He will carry you in the shelter of His wings and one day He will set you upon high ground. When that day comes you will look back and say, "Yes Lord, I can see how You carried me. I can see how You delivered me. I can see how very much You loved me in the gifts and miracles You laid at my feet when I couldn't even feel Your presence; when I didn't even know You were there." Believe in Jesus. Read His Word. Commune with Him. If you allow Him, He will direct your path.

I don't think we ever totally get over the dreadfully agonizing losses we experience in this life but I do believe we get through them. Find comfort in knowing that God will send friends, loved ones and circumstances to remind you that you are not alone in your sorrow. Your friends are willing to grieve with you, cry with you and pray with you. At times they will admonish or correct you but know that it is done out of their concern and deep love for you.

On that day when you unwaveringly realize that you have not only survived your heartache but surrendered your will to the One who will direct your new life, those same friends will proudly stand at your side and openly rejoice with you. He does have a plan for your life, dear one - a plan for your future, to prosper you, to fill you with promise and with hope. Perhaps I repeat these words to you because it took me so long to accept them as truth for me. But true they are - they are promises intended every bit as much for you as they were for me.

Once you have come through the worst of your trials you will look back and humbly give thanks to the Lord for all that you have learned. You will graciously appreciate those friends who stood by you and contemplate with wonderment how they were able to survive your constant cries for help and your unending pleas of neediness. You will find that

God will bless them for their faithfulness. You will see God in the compassion of your friend's eyes, their gift of prayers and their commitment to walk with you along your jagged path of broken dreams, through your loss, your pain and into your place of healing and wholeness.

You will learn as you humble yourself before the Lord that He will use your humility not only to bless you but He will give you an opportunity to bless others too. You will discover that you are no longer limited by your loss but seasoned and strong. You will see the many ways in which God expressed His love for you even on the days you were unable to feel His presence. You will find that He was listening all along. You will see that in the darkest days of your anguish it was God's love that carried you through.

Remember dear one, God's healing grace sometimes comes to us in very unusual ways. He shows Himself through prayers we may never know were uttered, through unexpected acts of kindness, or in reminding us of special memories hidden away in the recesses of our mind. He comes in great acts of generosity and simple acts of love. And sometimes, yes, sometimes, God comes to us through a faithful friend with a little black dress. ❤

God Bless You, Heal You and Keep You Safe -
May God's Love, Joy, and Peace Remain
Always in Your Heart.
In His Love, Robyn ❤

"Gracious words are a honeycomb,
sweet to the soul and healing to the bones."
Proverbs 16:24
NIV

♥ ♥ ♥ ♥ ♥ ♥ ♥ ♥ ♥ ♥ ♥ ♥ ♥ ♥ ♥ ♥ ♥ ♥ ♥ ♥

Jesus,
My Wound Healer

I was wounded;
Jesus was wounded for our transgressions.
I was betrayed;
Jesus was betrayed for 30 pieces of silver.
I was forgotten;
Jesus said I will never leave you or forsake you.
I was broken hearted;
Jesus was broken for the sins of the world.
I felt lost;
Jesus said, "My sheep hear My voice."
I felt unworthy;
Jesus said, "Worthy is the Lamb."
I said, "I need peace, Lord."
Jesus said, "I am your peace, My peace I give unto you,
My peace I leave with you."
I cried;
Jesus wept.
I pled for mercy;
Jesus said, "I am the way, the truth and the light."
I said, "Lord, give me new life."
Jesus said, "I give you life and have given it more
abundantly."
I said, "Jesus, have I forgotten these things? Forgive
me."
Jesus said, "I already have….."

Robyn B. Light

- 2008 -

♥ ♥ ♥ ♥ ♥ ♥ ♥ ♥ ♥ ♥ ♥ ♥ ♥ ♥ ♥ ♥ ♥ ♥ ♥ ♥

Appendix

The following pages contain materials to help guide you through your own little black dress party.

- ❤ Sample Invitation Card
  - Front Cover
  - Inside Invitation (left side of card)
  - Inside Invitation (right side of card)
- ❤ Guest List
- ❤ Party Plans
- ❤ Thank You Card
  - Front Cover
  - Inside Invitation (left side of card)
  - Inside Invitation (right side of card)

"The Little Black Dress Party"

An Evening of Reflection and Prayer.

"The Little Black Dress"
❧ Wounded Heart ~ Healing God ☙

A Book Reading

"A friend loveth at all times…"
Proverbs 17:17(a)
KJV

It's time for an evening filled with friendship and reflection.

*Dress up in your favorite little black dress
and come join us!*

What:	**Book Reading & Potluck**
Where:	
Date:	**Time:**
RSVP	
Name:	**Number:**
Name:	**Number:**

*Bring your favorite main dish, appetizer or dessert.
Beverages will be provided.*

Guest List

❤ ❤ ❤ ❤ ❤ ❤ ❤ ❤ ❤ ❤ ❤ ❤ ❤ ❤ ❤ ❤ ❤ ❤

NAME   *PHONE #/EMAIL*   *POTLUCK ITEM*

_____

_____

_____

_____

_____

_____

_____

_____

_____

_____

_____

_____

_____

_____

❤ ❤ ❤ ❤ ❤ ❤ ❤ ❤ ❤ ❤ ❤ ❤ ❤ ❤ ❤ ❤ ❤ ❤

Party Plans

♥ ♥

1. Choose the date and location of your party.
2. Create your invitations and select the women you
    would like to invite. Smaller groups are best unless
    you plan on breaking into small groups later for the
    purpose of discussion and prayer.
3. Keep a list of guests and what potluck item they plan
    to bring to the party.
4. Select a woman to do the book reading. (You may
    select two women if you prefer, however the reading
    works best with no more than two readers.)
5. First, enjoy your potluck and allow the women to
    visit and get to know those they may be meeting for
    the first time. This also provides ample time for those
    who know each other to catch up with what's going
    on in their lives.
6. Finish your meal and proceed with a brief
    introduction of the book. The reading may include
    only the first portion of the book, "The Little Black
    Dress," or the book in its entirety.
7. Allow time for discussion following the book reading.
    (You may want to have a series of no more than five
    questions to present to the group). Here are some
    ideas for questions to ask:

    a. What were some of the thoughts, feelings
        or reactions described in the book that you
        too have experienced? Encourage sharing by
        asking those who may feel more comfortable
        to begin the discussion by sharing some of
        their experiences and grief history.

b. A broken relationship can be a very painful experience. What were some of the things you did to help yourself get past the grief and move on from your loss?

c. What is one positive thing you learned from your painful experience?

d. What healing words could you pass on to others who are not as far along in their healing process?

e. Generally all of us have experienced a crisis or a traumatic event in our lives. Was there anything someone did for you during this difficult time that was especially meaningful? What could others have done that would have been of help to you?

f. Share a favorite Scripture, thought or quote that helped you overcome your feelings of loss, grief or despair.

8. Make sure you have a camera and take a photograph of the group. Commit to sending a copy of the photograph to each woman in attendance.

9. Beforehand, select a woman to close the evening in prayer. Advise the group there will be women available to pray with them. (Some women may need special attention or personal prayer.) Encourage them to stay in touch. A supportive friend makes all the difference!

10. Send thank cards to those who attended and enclose a copy of the photograph from the little black dress party.

❤ ❤ ❤ ❤ ❤ ❤ ❤ ❤ ❤ ❤ ❤ ❤ ❤ ❤ ❤ ❤ ❤ ❤ ❤

"The Little Black Dress Party" ❤

Thank You for Joining Us!

thelittleblackdressbookbyrobyn@yahoo.com

Robyn B. Light
Post Office Box 2484
Yakima, Washington 98907

Thank you for attending the little black dress party!
We were privileged to share the evening with you.

Enclosed please find your copy of the
little black dress photograph.

May the Lord bless you and keep you,

The Little Black Dress – Quotes from Friends:

"This is a story of a friend's heart - feeling, giving and loving." Linda B.

"Robyn is like a daughter to me. I know her tender heart and I know her love for the Lord. My heart broke to see her in so much pain but my spirit rejoiced when I saw her allow the Lord to change and renew her life. Even as a woman who is now in her 80's this book spoke to me in so many ways. I know it will bless others as it blessed me." Donna P.

"This is a precious story of God's love demonstrated in the simplest yet most powerful of forms – friendship. Very touching – the perfect read for anyone who knows the pain of a broken heart." Vonda G.

"Robyn has captured the essence of healing from the inside out! Through faith and friendship, Robyn was able to restore the direction of her future and rekindle the passion within her self! A journey of grieving to believing!" Gloria H.

"If you have loved and lost before, feel sad, hopeless, or alone, this book packs a spiritual wallop that will point you to a new awakening in your relationship with Christ." Rhonda S.

"This is a poignant, beautiful story about the power of friendship and how one friend helped another through a great time of sadness over a broken relationship. Ultimately sustaining faith wins over and the healing begins. This book is a must read for every women!" Lonna B.

"This book spoke to me because I too have a special friend who helped me thru a very difficult period in my life. Thank you Robyn for the courage to share your story – I know it will help many other women who have felt the pain of a similar loss." Arlene F.

One woman's experience during a life changing sadness illustrates that by entering a world of "dress up," even for a moment, the course can be altered and the chains of great sorrow broken. This book puts words to the pain of emotions involved in an affair of the greatest idol maker, our heart. Donna F.

"God will use us.... we just have to allow Him to." Thelma B.

"Discovering a group of women, who had not met before the reading of "The Little Black Dress," was quite an extraordinary experience. After the reading I realized we all had a common thread; something in our backgrounds had brought us together. Each had a story to tell. Robyn has captured that moment here." Pam B.

"While all of us may not have a little black dress to deliver to the front door of a hurting friend we can deliver this book. Along with it we can bring our loving words of encouragement, our support and our prayers. This book will help and bless many." Gail B.

"Our Blessed Father uses Robyn to express His love for us in a truly communal way. She was open to receiving Gods Word for her life and then expressing her experience in a way that uniquely melds with our hearts. She tells her story of heartbreak and devastation, and how God used the bond of Christian sisterhood for blessed healing." Vickie D.

A native of Washington State, Robyn B. Light spent her professional career working in the criminal justice system as a law enforcement officer, crime victim services manager and senior investigator for the local prosecuting attorney's office. She has been a founding member of a number of crime victim services and a long standing member of the National Organization for Victim Assistance. Ms. Light serves on their national crisis response team. As a CRT member she has responded to a number of our nations most  catastrophic events including the Oklahoma City bombing in 1985 and to the states of New York and New Jersey following the tragic events of September 11th, 2001. Ms. Light has been a leader in the field of crime victim services on a local, state and national level. She has written a number of training materials related to crime victimization; maintains a private consulting firm, is a master trainer for NOVA and continues to serve the crime victims of her state as a community victim liaison. Among other legislative endeavors Ms. Light authored the first Child Victims Bill of Rights in Washington State which was unanimously enacted into law in 1985. She previously wrote a book for helping children through the criminal justice system called, "When Kids Testify In Court." She has been the recipient of a number of local, state and national awards for her groundbreaking work in the field of victim services and critical incident response. She believes life's sweetest pleasures are found in enjoying time with family, friends, and her two Doberman Pinschers, Micah and Asya. Her faith in Jesus Christ is the cornerstone of her life and she believes there is no greater gift than knowing and serving Him.

The Little Black Dress
Wounded Heart ~ Healing God

Contact information:

thelittleblackdressbookbyrobyn@yahoo.com

Robyn B. Light
Post Office Box 2484
Yakima, Washington 98907